COLORADO

THE CENTENNIAL STATE

Population: **4.3 million and growing**

Area: **104,247 sq. miles; 8th largest state**

Capital: **Denver**

To enter the union: **38th on August 1, 1876, thus the nickname**

Highest point: **14,433', Mt. Elbert near Leadville**

Lowest point: **3,350' on the Arkansas River at the Kansas line**

Time zone: **Mountain time**

Highest state in the nation: **54 peaks over 14,000' above sea level**

Major industries: **tourism and recreation; agriculture (ranching and farming); natural resources (oil & gas, and minerals mining); high technology manufacturing.**

Tree: **Colorado Blue Spruce**

Flower: **Columbine**

Bird: **Lark Bunting**

Animal: **Bighorn Sheep**

Fossil: **Stegosaurus**

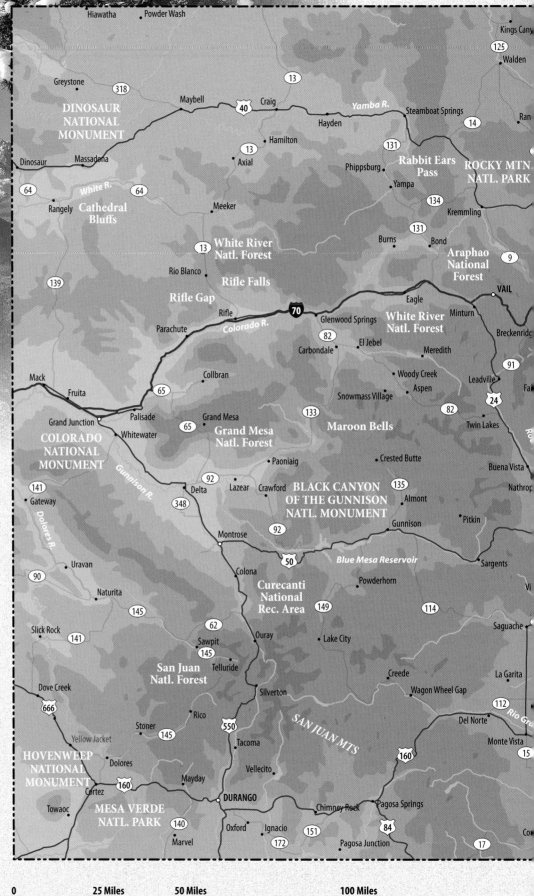

Map Legend

★ State Capital

● Cities 100,000-499,999

● Cities 50,000-99,999

○ Cities 10,000-49,999

· Cities 0-9,999

- - - State Boundaries

━ Interstate Highways

━ U.S. Highways

◯ State roads

≈ Rivers and lakes

- 12000+ Ft.
- 9000-12000 Ft.
- 7500-9000 Ft.
- 6000-7500 Ft.
- 4500-6000 Ft.
- 3000-4500 Ft.
- 1800-3000 Ft.

Compass: N, W, E, S

Map labels

Hiawatha · Powder Wash · Kings Cany
Greystone · 318 · Maybell · 40 · Craig · Yampa R. · Steamboat Springs · 14 · 125 · Walden · Ran

DINOSAUR NATIONAL MONUMENT
Dinosaur · Massadona · 13 · Hamilton · Hayden
13 · Axial · Phippsburg · Rabbit Ears Pass · 131 · ROCKY MTN. NATL. PARK
64 · 64 · White R. · Yampa · 134
Rangely · Cathedral Bluffs · Meeker · 131 · Kremmling
13 · White River Natl. Forest · Burns · Bond · Araphao National Forest · 9
139 · Rio Blanco · Rifle Falls · Eagle · VAIL
Rifle Gap · 70 · Glenwood Springs · White River Natl. Forest · Minturn
Rifle · Colorado R. · Breckenridge
Parachute · 82 · El Jebel · Meredith · 91
Mack · Collbran · Carbondale · Woody Creek · Leadville · Fa
Fruita · 65 · Grand Mesa · Snowmass Village · Aspen · 82 · 24
Grand Junction · 65 · Grand Mesa Natl. Forest · 133 · Maroon Bells · Twin Lakes · Ro
Palisade · COLORADO NATIONAL MONUMENT · Whitewater · Paoniaig · Crested Butte · Buena Vista
141 · Gunnison R. · 92 · Lazear · Crawford · BLACK CANYON OF THE GUNNISON NATL. MONUMENT · 135 · Nathrop
Gateway · Delta · Almont
Dolores R. · 348 · Gunnison · Pitkin
90 · Montrose · 92 · Blue Mesa Reservoir · Sargents
Uravan · 50 · Colona · Powderhorn · Vi
Naturita · Curecanti National Rec. Area · 149 · 114 · Saguache
145 · 62 · Ouray · Lake City · Creede · La Garita
Slick Rock · Sawpit · 145 · San Juan Natl. Forest · Telluride · Wagon Wheel Gap · 112
141 · Silverton · SAN JUAN MTS · Del Norte · Rio Gr
Dove Creek · Rico · 550 · Monte Vista
666 · Stoner · 145 · Tacoma · 160 · 15
Yellow Jacket · HOVENWEEP NATIONAL MONUMENT · Dolores · Mayday · Vellecito · Chimney Rock · Pagosa Springs
Cortez · 160 · DURANGO · 84
Towaoc · MESA VERDE NATL. PARK · 140 · Oxford · Ignacio · 151 · Pagosa Junction · 17 · Co
Marvel · 172

Scale

| 0 | 25 Miles | 50 Miles | 100 Miles |

| 0 | 25 Km | 50 Km | 100 Km |

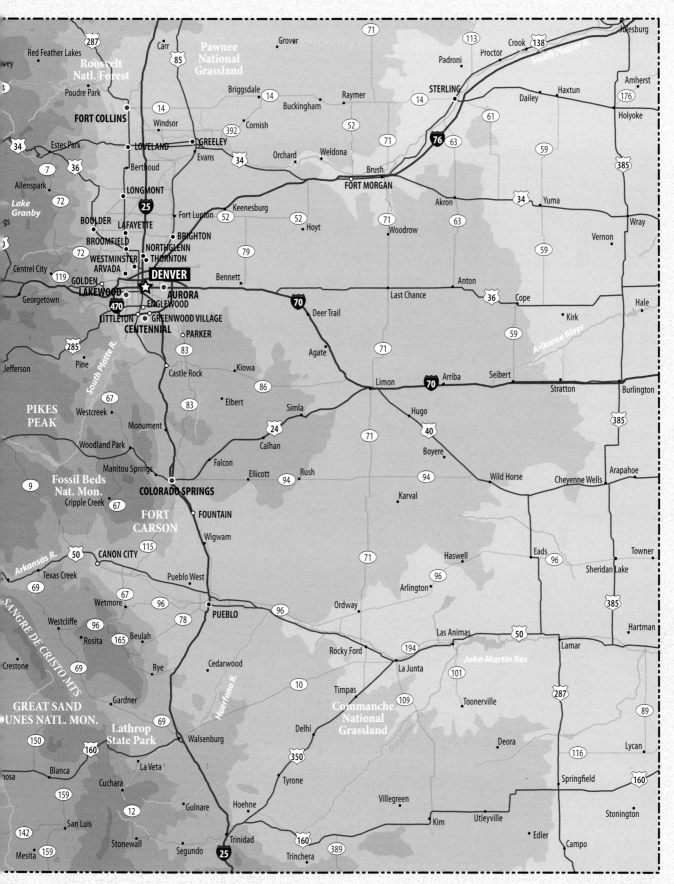

COLORADO MAP

The Colorado flag consists of blue stripes for bright blue skies, white for snow-capped mountains, red for rock formations, and yellow for the brilliant sunshine.

INTRODUCTION

Welcome to colorful Colorado. The state's name comes from the Spanish word meaning red, the name first given to the Colorado River which is colored from eroding red sandstone cliffs. Colorado, the highest state in the union (3,350' at its lowest point and 14,433' at its highest), contains large sections of the Great Plains and the Rocky Mountains and is divided from north to south by the Continental Divide. Flat plains constitute 40% of the state's land mass, mountains 40%, and high plateaus the remaining 20%.

Eastern Colorado is primarily agricultural with irrigated and dry land farms producing wheat, corn, sugar beets, melons and potatoes. Ranches throughout the state raise cattle, sheep and buffalo. Western Colorado contains high peaks, green valleys, deep gorges and plateaus. From the fertile lower Gunnison and Colorado River valleys, fruit orchards support local trade.

America's best known mountain, Pikes Peak, near Colorado Springs, and Longs Peak, in Rocky Mountain National Park, are just two of the 54 peaks in the state over 14,000' above sea level. Katharine Lee Bates composed America The Beautiful after visiting the "purple mountain majesties" of Pikes Peak. Spectacular rock formations abound, in the red sandstone of the Garden of the Gods near Colorado Springs, in the Royal Gorge on the Arkansas River, and in the dark granite of the Black Canyon of the Gunnison River. Starting high in the Rocky Mountains and slicing through the state, rivers for recreation, scenic beauty, irrigation, and municipal drinking water flow east and west from the Continental Divide.

Early Colorado was populated by Indian tribes including the Arapaho, Cheyenne, Comanche, Kiowa, Shoshone, Ute, and Navajo. Magnificent cliff dwellings over 1000 years old from the Anasazi tribes, an ancestor of the Pueblos, can be visited in Mesa Verde National Park in the southwestern corner of the state. Take along your courage and your walking shoes and climb into some of these magnificent aerial apartments.

From the 1600's, evidence remains of Spanish explorers looking for gold, in many southern parts of the state. In 1803, Colorado officially became part of the United States with the Louisiana Purchase at 4 cents per acre, and was made a state in 1876. In the 1840's and 50's, the discovery of gold lured miners and entrepreneurs to seek their fortunes. Colorado mines still produce gold, silver and molybdenum. Seventy-five percent of the nation's oil shale reserves are in Colorado. Petroleum and natural gas are Colorado's most important natural resources. The nation's only operating diamond mine is north of Ft. Collins, near the Wyoming border. Recently, a 26+ carat diamond was extracted from there. Throughout the state, scattered gold mines are open to the public. A restored mining town, Old Colorado City, in Fairplay offers a fascinating window into the past. Try your luck gold panning in our rivers or put on a hard hat and venture deep into one of the mines where guides help you go back in time 140 years.

Today, recreation, entertainment and tourism are major industries in all 4 seasons. Colorado is renown for deer, elk, bear, antelope, duck, goose, pheasant and grouse hunting, and for fishing in prime wild

For purple mountain majesties above the fruited plain...

rivers and streams. Dozens of ski areas for downhill and cross country offer some of the finest powder trails in the world. White water rafting, camping, back packing, rock and mountain climbing are other popular sports. For the armchair athlete, Colorado hosts several major league professional teams, including the Denver Broncos, Denver Nuggets, Colorado Avalanche, Colorado Rockies, Colorado Rapids and Colorado Mammoth.

Enjoy your visit to Colorado. The sun shines 300 days a year here. The low humidity virtually guarantees pleasant travels, no matter what the season.

Oh beautiful
for spacious skies...

CONTENTS

DENVER

Denver, the capital of Colorado, is known as the Mile High City because of its elevation of 5,280'. It sits at the base of the foothills of the Rocky Mountains. Denver was settled in 1858 by gold rushers and was a brawling, dusty frontier town. The Capitol building's dome is covered in gold leaf from Colorado mines.

Early gold panners were disappointed at the poor yields from local creeks. Many went home broke. Denver subsequently became a gambling and pleasure center, with a secret tunnel under a street linking one of the older hotels with a nearby brothel. Denver's economy has always been up and down, in the early days linked to mining discoveries and in more recent years dependent on fossil fuels and other energy sources.

Today the city is a multi-national mecca with a mix of many ethnicities.

Besides the theater arts center, Denver has an art museum, a natural history museum and a western history museum. It has a huge system of mountain parks, covering over 14,000 acres in the foothills.

Denver sports fans are some of the most avid in the country. Professional football, basketball, baseball and hockey boast sell-out crowds for most games. In January, Denver hosts the National Western Stock Show and Rodeo which also draws large crowds and connects the city to its western heritage.

► Colorado's State Capitol Building in gold leaf splendor

▼ Downtown Denver skyline from Civic Center Park, in mid-summer beauty

◄ Coors Field, home of the Colorado Rockies, in Lower Downtown (LoDo)

► Invesco Field at Mile High, home of the Denver Broncos

BE SURE TO SEE:

**16th Street Mall
and the Tabor Center**

Larimer Square
Flavor of the late 1800's

**LoDo (lower downtown)
and Coors Field**
Home of the Colorado Rockies

Invesco Field @ Mile High
Home of the Denver Broncos

DIA
The nation's and the world's
international airport
for the 21st century

Denver Zoo
3000 animals from 600 species

Museum of Nature & Science

Denver Library

Performing Arts Complex
One of the nation's largest
with several theaters

Six Flags Elitch Gardens
Amusement park

▲ Downtown Denver with State
Capitol in background

◄ The Denver Center for the Performing Arts complex

Denver skyline at night

Denver International Airport

THE FOOTHILLS

Historic Central City, Colorado, once home to miners in search of gold, is now a place to shop, gamble, see a good opera or merely step back in time and relish the past.

▼ The Mountain community of Nederland, Colorado, with the Eldora Ski Area in the background

The Flatirons near Boulder

Boulder, home of the University of Colorado, is approximately 25 miles northwest of Denver. Settled in 1876, it is now a high tech center similar to Silicon Valley in California. Boulder is a rich mixture of urban and rural geography incorporating a 5,000 acre system of parks and trails into its surroundings. The world's only municipal-owned glacier, Arapahoe Glacier provides drinking water to the city.

The rock formations outside of Boulder, called the Flatirons, were named by early settlers because they resemble irons used for pressing which were heated on wood stoves.

Red Rocks Park, just west of Denver, is a 10,000 seat natural amphitheater from red sandstone formations created more than 1 million years ago. It hosts a wide variety of classical and popular concerts during the summer months.

▼ Red Rocks Park at Easter sunrise

ESTES PARK

E stes Park, population 3,200, is a charming mountain community at the entrance to Rocky Mountain National Park. It has many tourist shops, restaurants and lodgings for park visitors.

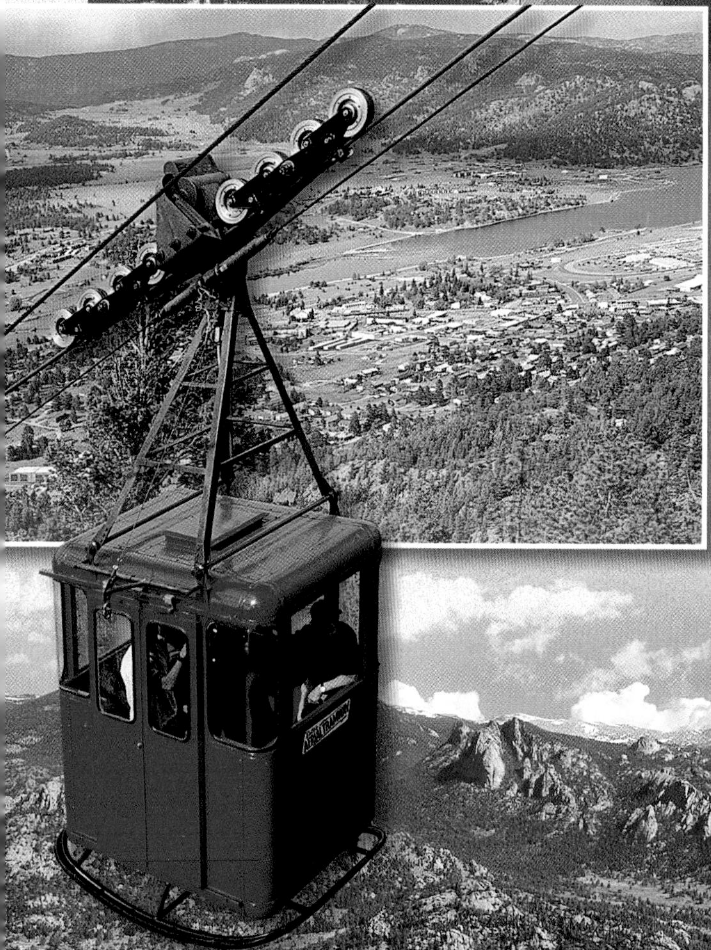

◀ Cable car at Estes Park

▼ An overview of beautiful Estes Park

The Stanley Hotel

Opened in 1909, this historic hotel in Estes Park, was built by F.O. Stanley who co-invented the Stanley Steamer. The hotel was the site of filming for Stephen King's mini-series, "The Shining".

ROCKY MOUNTAIN NATIONAL PARK

◄ Longs Peak and Autumn's golden Aspen

▲ Longs Peak, elevation 14,255', from Trail Ridge Road in Rocky Mountain National Park

▼ Pagoda Mountain

Rocky Mountain National Park lies 60 miles northwest of Denver and offers towering peaks, sculptured mountain valleys, wild, plunging icy-cold streams and dense forests interlaced with Ponderosa and Lodgepole pines, Blue Spruce and quaking Aspen. At the higher elevations, above treeline, vast acres of Alpine tundra (uncommon outside the Arctic) with its fragile eco-system can be viewed.

The park contains 410 sq. miles-265,193 acres with elevations ranging from 7,640' to 14,256'.

Many miles of trails exist for hikers from tenderfoots to the seasoned. Wildlife is plentiful-elk, deer, moose, mountain lion, coyote, big-horn sheep and black bear. Trail Ridge Road, once a trail used by the Utes and Arapahoes, offers scenic vistas including majestic plateaus, lush meadows and many of the 107 peaks in the park over 11,000' elevation.

▲ Mills Lake

▲ Diamond Face, Longs Peak, at sunrise

◄ One of the many riding trails in Rocky Mountain National Park

▼ Sprague Lake

▼ An extraordinary sunset captured in Rocky Mountain National Park

Haynach Lakes ▲

▲ Hallet Peak, 12,713', Rocky Mountain National Park

Trail Ridge Road, in early June, over the Continental Divide, through Rocky Mountain National Park ▶

Trail Ridge Road ▼

COLORADO SPRINGS

Colorado Springs (elevation 5,980') is the state's second largest city. It was founded in 1871 as a Denver and Rio Grande Railroad center and offered a playground for the wealthy. Colorado Springs boasts 250 sunny days a year. In the Cripple Creek area of the 1890's over $300 million in gold ore was mined. Today Colorado Springs is the home of the North American Air Defense Command (NORAD) buried in the granite of Cheyenne Mountain, several military bases, and the U.S. Olympic Training Center.

▼ Pioneers Museum

▼ Colorado Springs skyline at the foot of Pikes Peak, 14,115'

◄ Shrine of the Sun (Will Rogers)

▼ Fort Carson, United States Army Post

FORT CARSON
COLORADO
THE MOUNTAIN POST

◄ Seven Falls

▼ Downtown

BE SURE TO SEE:

United States Air Force Academy™, The Broadmoor Hotel, Garden of the Gods Trading Post and Visitors Center, Pikes Peak, Seven Falls, Cave of the Winds, Flying W Ranch, Ghost Town, Pioneers Museum, and the Rocky Mountain Dinosaur Resource Center.

BE SURE TO SEE:

The several statues
including a B-52 bomber

Scenic overlooks

The planetarium

Falcon Stadium

The noon meal
Cadet Formation

The Chapel

The wildlife

The United States Air Force Academy™, the youngest of the four service academies, trains men and women for careers in the Air Force. The campus contains 17,000 acres and houses 4,500 cadets. Many buildings are open to the public. Do not miss the beautiful 17-spired Cadet Chapel, an all faith center of worship.

UNITED STATES

▲ A-10 Warthog display

▲ Air Force Academy Chapel

AIR FORCE ACADEMY™

THE BROADMOOR
COLORADO SPRINGS

A Five Star Hotel

For a complete list of resort
services, amenities and activities,
visit: **www.broadmoor.com**

PIKES PEAK

Pikes Peak's summit can be reached by car, on foot, or by the cog railway. Atop the summit, Denver is visible 75 miles to the north and the Sangre de Cristo Mountain Range is visible 100 miles to the south.

▲ Pikes Peak as seen from Garden of the Gods

◄ Cog railroad on Pikes Peak

The view from America's most famous mountain is staggering in its immensity. This inspired Katharine Lee Bates to write her poem which, later set to music, became our unofficial national anthem, "America the Beautiful".

"Pikes Peak or Bust" was the cry of the gold seekers as they headed West to find their fortunes in Colorado's mountains. Few found riches, but all found a land of contrasting beauty and a healthful climate. Located in an alpine-desert environment, at an altitude of more than 6,000 feet, Colorado Springs enjoys moderate temperatures and low humidity. The days are generally sunny and the nights are cool and comfortable.

SUMMIT
PIKES PEAK
ALTITUDE 14,115 FT.

CITY OF COLORADO SPRINGS
PIKES PEAK HIGHWAY

MANITOU
COG WHEEL ROUTE
PIKES PEAK

A SUMMIT PHOTO IS A LASTING MEMENTO OF
YOUR TRIP TO THIS WORLD-FAMOUS PEAK

GARDEN OF THE GODS

Towering spires of red sandstone
in the Garden of the Gods

Garden of the Gods

Garden of the Gods Visitors Center

Garden of the Gods is a national natural landmark boasting giant, striking red and white limestone formations including Cathedral Rock, Balanced Rock and Kissing Camels. These vertical formations occurred from gigantic forces tilting the horizontal sedimentary layers upward. The red color is particularly striking at sunrise and sunset.

Various rock formations

The Siamese Twins

Balanced Rock

MANITOU SPRINGS

▼ Downtown Manitou Springs

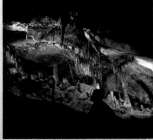

Manitou Springs (elevation 6,336'), sits at the foot of Pikes Peak, just west of Colorado Springs. It is best known for the iron and soda natural springs which led Manitou to becoming a natural health spa area. Nearby lies the Cave of the Winds with miles of tunnels exposing stalagmites and stalactites. A 40 minute walking tour wanders through 20 rooms on a paved, well-lighted trail. The cliff dwellings recreate the architectural dwellings of the great Pueblo period. In the summer, Indian dances can be seen daily.

▲ Miramont Castle overlooks Manitou Springs   ▲ The Cave of the Winds

▲ Cliff Dwellings near Manitou Springs

▼► Cripple Creek, from gold mining to casino gambling

The Royal Gorge Bridge, 8 miles west off US 50 outside Cañon City, is the world's highest suspension bridge. It spans 1,053' above the Arkansas River. A 3 mile paved, one way road traverses the ridge and offers breath-taking views.

ROYAL GORGE

Train rides on the Cañon City & Royal Gorge Railroad pass through the spectacular scenery of the Royal Gorge and under the world highest suspension bridge.

▼ Royal Gorge incline from rim to Arkansas River, 1053' below

GREAT SAND DUNES
NATIONAL PARK AND PRESERVE

The Great Sand Dunes is a 38,000 acre National Park and Preserve. Accumulating over 15,000 years, sand, too heavy to be carried by the wind over the mountains, forms an ever-changing foreground. Local legends claim entire wagon trains have disappeared in the dunes, and claim unusual creatures hide behind the shifting mounds. The highest dunes are over 700'.

Views of the Great Sand Dunes, near Alamosa

GREAT SAND DUNES
NATIONAL PARK AND PRESERVE

NATIONAL PARK SERVICE
DEPARTMENT OF THE INTERIOR

Cumbres and Toltec Railroad is America's longest and highest narrow-gauge railroad between Antonito, Colorado (south of Alamosa) and Chama, New Mexico . An all day trip on the coal burning train offers spectacular views of the Sangre de Cristo (Blood of Christ) and the San Juan mountain ranges.

CUMBRES & TOLTEC RAILROAD

▼ ▶ The narrow-gauge Cumbres and Toltec Railroad

... TO THE DIVIDE

▲ Drivers are treated to a spectacular view of the Continental Divide on I-70 at the Genesee Bridge, near the Buffalo Herd Overlook, just 20 miles from Denver

Idaho Springs-Mt. Evans. The Ute Indians first used these mineral springs for healing purposes. After the gold rush of the 1850's, exhausted miners soothed their aches in the springs. Today, skiers and hikers stop for a refreshing soak and swim. More than 200 mines continue to operate in the area producing silver, uranium, tungsten, zinc, molybdenum, gold and lead. Many Victorian buildings still stand.

A popular drive loops from Idaho Springs through Chicago Creek Canyon, past Echo Lake and Mt. Evans, over Squaw Pass to Bergen Park and back to I-70. Mountain goats are a frequent sight atop Mt. Evans along with spectacular views of Denver and the plains to the east and the Rockies to the west.

▼ Charles Tayler Water Wheel, Idaho Springs

Argo Gold Mill museum, Idaho Springs ▼

IDAHO SPRINGS

MOUNT EVANS

▲▼ Mt. Evans and Echo Lake

Idaho Springs, 40 miles west of Denver on I-70 ▶

A view of Mt. Evans in late winter

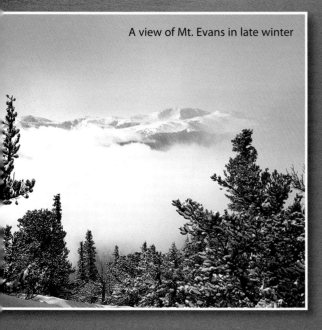

COLORADO SEASONS

Colorado's climate and altitude combine to create seasons of sensual splendor. Winter provides the mountains with plentiful powder for excellent skiing, snowboarding and other activities. Warm, sun-filled Spring days can quickly melt the snowpack bringing the colorful array of mountain wildflowers. Summer brings long hot, dry days good for camping, hiking, biking and brilliant sunsets. Crisp, cool nights in Autumn help turn the quaking aspen into mountains of orange and gold. Because of the altitude, the sun is brighter here, the sky is bluer, the air is drier. Colorado seasons can also be fickle- it can be 75 degrees in Denver in January, while it can snow in June. The mountains also play games- Denver can get three feet of snow in March, while it can be near 70 degrees in Vail. Whatever the season, Colorado offers spectacular beauty and ample opportunity for fun and recreation throughout the year.

Mount of the Holy Cross 14,005' as seen from the top of Vail ski area at sunrise. Can you find the cross?

◀ Maxwell House, Georgetown

GEORGETOWN

Georgetown, called the Silver Queen by early settlers, at one time was the 3rd largest city in the state. Initially miners rushed to Georgetown looking for gold which quickly ran out, emptying the town only to be reborn several years later, as a silver center. Today a 1920's narrow gauge railroad runs from Georgetown to Silver Plume with a stop along the way to visit the 1870's Lebanon Silver Mine.

Georgetown is a picturesque Victorian village with many shops and restaurants. Georgetown Lake outside town is a good wildlife viewing area especially for big horn sheep.

Georgetown holds its old-fashioned Christmas Market the first two weekends in December.

▼ I-70 to the east portal of Eisenhower
Tunnel, under the Continental Divide

▼ Sangre de Cristo Range

COLORADO FOURTEENERS

Colorado has 54 peaks over 14,000 feet high. The record for climbing all 54 peaks is under 16 days.

FRONT RANGE

Longs Peak	14,255
Mount Evans	14,264
Mount Bierstadt	14,060
Torreys Peak	14,267
Grays Peak	14,270
Pikes Peak	14,110

TEN MILE RANGE

Quandary Peak	14,265

MOSQUITO RANGE

Mount Lincoln	14,286
Mount Bross	14,172
Mount Democrat	14,148
Mount Sherman	14,036

SAWATCH RANGE

Mt. of the Holy Cross	14,005
Mount Massive	14,421
Mount Elbert	14,433
La Plata Peak	14,336
Mount Oxford	14,153
Mount Belford	14,197
Missouri Mountain	14,067
Huron Peak	14,005
Mount Harvard	14,420
Mount Columbia	14,073
Mount Yale	14,196
Mount Princeton	14,197
Mount Antero	14,269
Tabeguache Mountain	14,155
Mount Shavano	14,229

ELK RANGE

Castle Peak	14,265
Pyramid Peak	14,018
North Maroon Peak	14,014
Maroon Peak	14,156
Capitol Peak	14,130
Snowmass Mountain	14,092

SANGRE DE CRISTO RANGE

Kit Carson Peak	14,165
Humboldt Peak	14,064
Crestone Peak	14,294
Crestone Needle	14,197
Mount Lindsey	14,042
Ellingwood Peak	14,042
Blanca Peak	14,345
Little Bear Peak	14,037
Culebra Peak	14,047

SAN JUAN RANGE

San Luis Peak	14,014
Uncompahgre Peak	14,309
Wetterhorn Peak	14,015
Redcloud Peak	14,034
Sunshine Peak	14,001
Handies Peak	14,048

NEEDLE MOUNTAINS

Sunlight Peak	14,059
Windom Peak	14,082
Mount Eolus	14,083

SNEFFELS RANGE

Mount Sneffels	14,150

SAN MIGUEL RANGE

Wilson Peak	14,017
Mount Wilson	14,246
El Diente Peak	14,159

Only Pike's Peak and Mt. Evans have automobile roads to the summit. The highest peak in the world is Mt. Everest in Asia at 29,028 feet. The tallest mountain in North America is Mt. McKinley, Alaska, which is 20,320 feet.

HIGH COUNTRY

▼ Sneffels Range

▲ Twilight Peak, San Juan Mountains, near Silverton

▼ San Juan Range, SW Colorado

▼ Maroon Bells, Aspen

▼ Snowmass Mountain, Aspen

SUMMIT COUNTY

Summit County is the home to 4 major ski areas-Keystone, Copper Mountain, Breckenridge and Arapahoe Basin. Outdoor recreation is available through all the seasons, with excellent boating and fishing on Dillon Reservoir. Sport enthusiasts enjoy hiking and biking along the paved trail from Breckenridge to Frisco to Vail. Other summer activities include music festivals, golf tournaments, mountain bike race series, film and hot air balloon festivals.

Gore Range, west of Dillon ▼ ▶

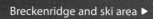

Lake Dillon

◀ Breckenridge at night

▼ Hoosier Pass astride the Continental Divide, between Fairplay and Breckenridge

HOOSIER PASS
ELEVATION 11,542 FEET

CONTINENTAL DIVIDE

ATLANTIC OCEAN
WATERSHED
SOUTH PLATTE RIVER
PIKE NATIONAL FOREST
SOUTH PARK RANGER DISTRICT
PARK COUNTY

PACIFIC OCEAN
WATERSHED
BLUE RIVER
ARAPAHO NATIONAL FOREST
DILLON RANGER DISTRICT
SUMMIT COUNTY

U. S. DEPARTMENT OF AGRICULTURE – FOREST SERVICE

◀ Copper Mountain ski area between Frisco and Vail on I-70

▼ Aerial view of Keystone in Summit County, Colorado

▲ Crystal clear mountain lake on Fremont Pass between Leadville and Copper Mountain

▲ Leadville

LEADVILLE

Leadville (elevation 10,188'), once a silver mining center, is the highest city in America. Settlers first came to Leadville for the gold in 1860 and within 4 months of its discovery, the city housed over 5,000 miners. Although gold was plentiful it was very difficult to extract from the heavy black sand, which later was found to be rich in silver.

Leadville had a second boom as a silver city. Mining continues to be a major industry today.

Leadville ▼ ▶

▲ An eerie, snowy Vail night

VAIL

Vail is the home of the largest ski mountain in the United States, and rated by many as America's #1 resort. Vail encompasses over 11 sq. miles of ski terrain. The alpine style town has become a year round recreation area. The town was developed by ski paratroopers who had trained in the area during World War II. Today, the Vail Institute offers musical and cultural programs from July-September.

▼ Town of Vail at base of ski area

▲ Vail Pass visitors stop

▼ Shrine pass near Vail

Vail at night

GLENWOOD SPRINGS

Hanging Lake, 1200' above the Glenwood Canyon floor

◀▼ Glenwood Canyon, the Colorado River and the engineering marvel of I-70

G lenwood Springs: Hot mineral springs and natural vapor caves have been popular since the Ute Indian days. Doc Holliday, a dentist and notorious gunslinger made his home here. Glenwood lies at the end of a scenic 18 mile stretch of I-70 through Glenwood Canyon, on the edge of the Colorado River where steep cliffs of red sandstone abut the highway.

The Glenwood Hot Springs Pool, the world's largest outdoor mineral hot pool, extending 2 blocks long, is a popular soaking spot for area skiers.

Glenwood Hot Springs

▲ Aspen Mountain gondola

▲ Christmas time in Aspen

ASPEN

Aspen sits at the upper end of the Roaring Fork Valley, at the foot of 12,095' Independence Pass. Initially founded as a silver mining town, today Aspen is an exclusive ski resort, home to 4 separate ski areas: Aspen Mountain, Snowmass Village, Aspen Highlands and Buttermilk/Tiehack Mountain. Maroon Bells outside Aspen is Colorado's most photographed mountain. Summer activities abound including the famed Aspen Music Festival. Aspen has and continues to offer a second home to many Hollywood notables. Two ghost towns, Ashcroft and Independence, are nearby.

▼ ▶ Aspen Mountain and summer wildflowers

▼ Independence Pass, east of Aspen

INDEPENDENCE PASS
Elevation 12,095 feet
CONTINENTAL DIVIDE

▲ Snowmass Village

Snowmass Village, founded as a ski-town in 1967, is 10 miles west of Aspen. Do not confuse it with Snowmass, a collection of ranches and houses on the backside of Aspen's largest mountain. Snowmass Village is an all season resort with as many summer activities as winter.

T he Hotel Jerome, one of the most famous lodging places in Aspen, is a renovated 1889 hotel furnished with lovely antiques and Victorian reproductions. It is celebrated for its continental cuisine.

▼ Hotel Jerome, Aspen

M aroon Bells, 10 miles outside of Aspen has a picnic area, fishing, camping and hiking trails. During the summer, vehicle traffic to the mountain is limited to campers with permits and the physically impaired. Regular bus service is available to those wishing to enjoy the beautiful setting. Spectacular Colorado wildflowers offer breath-taking fields of splendor in the early summer months, while brilliant patches of gold Aspen shimmer from the hillsides in the fall.

◀ Summer carriage rides, downtown Aspen

MAROON BELLS

▲ ▼ Maroon Bells and Maroon Lake

GRAND JUNCTION

◀ Downtown Grand Junction attractions

G rand Junction sits at the junction of the Colorado and Gunnison Rivers, where the railroads from Denver and Salt Lake City meet. These rivers nourish the fertile soil of the Grand Valley, the fruit farming region of Colorado. Nearby sits the Grand Mesa, the largest flat-topped mountain in the world.

The Colorado National Monument west of town offers spectacular evidence of the unusual effects of erosion on sandstone. Isolated monoliths and canyons over 1000' deep tease the eye. Juniper and Piñon Pine dot the hillsides. This area is hot and dry in summer, starkly beautiful with yucca blossoms and wildflowers in the spring.

COLORADO
NATIONAL MONUMENT

The sheer cliffs of the Black Canyon

BLACK CANYON OF THE GUNNISON

The Gunnison River runs wild through somber-colored PreCambrian rocks of the Black Canyon 2,425' below the canyon rim. Descent into the canyon by foot is extremely arduous.

Crested Butte began as a coal mining town in 1883. Today it is a major ski area. A number of buildings from the 1880's are still standing, including a 2 story outhouse. Crested Butte is said to be the mountain biking capital of the world.

Slate River

Kebler Pass

Virginia Basin

CRESTED BUTTE

▲ Downtown Telluride   ▲ Bridal Veil Falls south of Telluride

TELLURIDE

Telluride began as a gold and silver mining town in 1875. It was named for the non-metallic material called tellurium from which gold and silver ore was extracted. It sits at the base of a box canyon down which the 425' Bridal Veil Falls tumble.

Today, Telluride is a popular ski resort. In the summer, it hosts a number of renowned festivals including the Telluride Blue Grass Festival, The Hang Gliding Festival and a jazz and film festival.

▲ Town of Ouray

▲ One of many glacier and spring fed waterfalls

OURAY

Ouray was named for the Ute Indian Chief Ouray who frequented the area to enjoy the hot springs. In 1875 silver was discovered and later gold.

Today, the springs form the Ouray Hot Springs Pool which is open to the public. Ouray, claimed to be the jeep capital of the world, offers over 400 miles of off-road adventure to 4 wheelers.

The Million Dollar Highway, connecting Silverton and Ouray, is one of the nation's most spectacular auto routes.

Durango was originally a mining town and smelting center for the region's gold and silver mines. Today it is a center for ranching and recreation. Durango is the gateway to the San Juan Mountains which, because younger, appear rougher, more jagged and stark. Whitewater rafting on the Animas and Dolores Rivers is a popular summer sport. The Durango and Silverton Narrow Gauge Railroad, in continuous operation since 1882, is a popular tourist attraction.

▲▶ The Durango and Silverton Narrow Gauge Railroad, coal-fired, follows the Animas River through the San Juan National Forest. Operating since 1882

DURANGO & SILVERTON

Silverton began its history in 1871 with a major silver strike. Today it is a popular tourist attraction and movie set because of the false-fronted buildings along the infamous Blair Street, once known for its pleasure domes. Over 700 miles of jeep roads remain in the San Juan's, making Silverton a center for off-road excursions.

◀ Town of Silverton

The Durango and Silverton train in winter operations

▲ Town of Silverton

▶ Town of Durango

▶ The 1887 Victorian-styled Strater Hotel, Durango

▲ Wolf Creek

PAGOSA SPRINGS

Wolf Creek Pass, near Pagosa Springs, crosses the Continental Divide, from where water flows to either the Pacific Ocean or the Gulf of Mexico. The annual snowfall for the area exceeds 450 inches.

▶ Chimney Rock, San Juan National Forest, between Pagosa Springs and Durango

M esa Verde National Park houses the greatest concentration of Indian ruins in the nation and is one of the country's major archeological preserves. Mesa Verde is Spanish for "green table", a plateau top 2000' above the valley floor. It is richly forested with Juniper and Piñon Pine. The Anasazi (ancestors of the Pueblo Indians) built Kivas (ceremonial rooms) and cliff dwellings in the eroded alcoves of the cliffs. On the Indian Reservations at Four Corners, 4 states meet (Utah, Colorado, New Mexico, Arizona). Today oil exploration and tourism contribute to the economy.

▲▼ Anasazi Indian ruins, known as cliff dwellings, from the 12th and 13th centuries in Mesa Verde National Park.

MESA VERDE NATIONAL PARK

GHOST TOWNS

At one time, Colorado had more than 700 ghost towns, most remnants of the boom or bust mining history. A few of these old mining villages have been reborn and are now thriving communities, like Aspen and Fairplay. Most have slowly fallen into the ground, victim to harsh winters and the preying hands of relic collectors. Some have completely disappeared and their sites found only with extreme difficulty. Other towns remain which are partly ghost, where old buildings still stand vacant, intermingled with new thriving businesses. Some of these buildings have or will be restored. Breckenridge, Telluride and Georgetown are good examples. Only a few towns remain, true ghosts, with empty-eyed buildings lining the streets.

In the 1860's, gold was the big allure, giving way to silver in the 1870's. Silver and gold mining continued to thrive until 1893 when silver was demonetized and the Colorado mining industry nearly collapsed. Fortunately gold was discovered in Cripple Creek at that time so mining as an industry continued to survive.

▼ Animas Forks is located at timberline on the North Fork of the Animas River. This town once had 1500 people and a railroad which was operable until 1942.

▲ ▼ Ashcroft, once a busy mining town in the 1870's, at one time larger than the town of Aspen. Many structures still remain, restored by the Aspen Historical Society. Accessible all year.

Most of the mining camps began as gold camps. When the gold veins petered out, the town would grow dormant as increasing numbers of miners moved to more fertile areas. Years later prospectors might find silver or other ores in the old sites and the boom would be reborn. Associated industries flourished along with the mines—smelting, reduction works as well as shops, restaurants and saloons.

Most mining camps started as tent cities, followed fairly quickly by log cabins and more permanent dwellings, once a sawmill was packed in. Often the stores had false two-story fronts to convey the idea of prosperity and elegance, even though both were lacking in most of these overnight cities. Brick and stone buildings began to appear if the town continued to flourish. The architecture of the towns resembled the part of the country from which the miners hailed. Georgetown, for example, looks decidedly New England in style.

Fire was a constant threat to these early towns. Many were completely destroyed and rebuilt on the ashes. Gold Hill had a fire so ravenous, the town inhabitants were forced to hide in the mine shafts until it burned itself out.

The type of mining evolved over the years. The first prospectors panned stream and river beds. Later miners climbed higher, looking for exposed ore in the mountain sides. Lode mining came next, with shafts and tunnels dynamited and dug deep into the mountain. These ores are less pure, requiring mills for extraction.

Visiting these crumbling towns is a real pleasure. It does not take too much imagination to see a town as it must have been, or to convince yourself that you can hear the ghosts of long ago miners whispering secrets about gold, gold, gold.

▲▼ Alta, once a large town where workers from the nearby Gold King Mine lived, from the 1870's until 1945. Many buildings are still standing.

▲ Nevadaville, one mile from the popular gambling casino town, Central City. It is now inhabited and privately owned so it is not a true ghost town.

◄ Independence. On July 4, 1879, a rich strike of gold was found in the mountains 15 mi. east of Aspen by Billy Belden. He called the mine the Independence. Later a town sprang up around the mine and was named for the mine. When the town applied for a post office, the name conflicted with the town in Missouri, so the town was renamed Chipeta, after Chief Ouray's wife. Later the name of the town changed many times to Mammoth City, Mt. Hope, Farewell, Sparkill and finally back to Independence. The town is maintained by the Aspen Historical Society and is attended in the summer.

◄ Carson, an old mining town built in 2 parts, one on each side of the Continental Divide. The earliest settlement was built around a silver strike on the east side. Some years later, gold was discovered and a second village sprang up around the Bachelor Gold Mine.

Crystal City, named for the nearby Crystal River. In the 1880's it was a busy town with 500 inhabitants.

It is famous today for the Crystal Mill, which was a hydro-powered powerhouse for the nearby Sheep Mt. Tunnel. The town is privately owned and inhabited in the summer and fall.

*S*t. Elmo, what we most imagine a ghost town should look like. Privately owned and inhabited in the summer. A few hearty residents remain year round. The town was originally named Forest City and renamed St. Elmo in the 1880's, after a popular novel.

THE WILD

Because of the great diversity of the Colorado environment, more than 960 species of wildlife inhabit the state, from the tiny Hummingbird to the great Eagle, from the Chipmunk to the Moose.

Also discover some of the hundreds of commonly seen wildflowers, from the brilliant blue of the Colorado Columbine to the scarlet red of the Indian Paintbrush, from the miniatures in the tundra above treeline to the larger cousins of clover, gentian, phlox, lupine, vetch, lilies and even orchids, found in the high country forest, meadows and along rushing streams.

Mountain Lion cubs

▼ Bald Eagle, the American national emblem

▲ Elk

▲ Buffalo

▲ Moose

▲ Chipmunk

▼ Bighorn sheep

◄ Mountain goats

◀ Golden leaves of the Aspen, Wildflowers and a Colorado Blue Columbine

▲ Black bears

◀ Red Fox

▼ Elk wintering deep in an evergreen forest

Colorado Blue Columbine,
the state flower ▶

A western Colorado rancher's
meadow of wildflowers ▶

Indian Paintbrush ▼

Photos by: Aerial Exposure, Don Allan, James Blank, Art Bilstein, Don Campbell, Diane Cooper, Tony Eitzel, Don Hite, Virginia Karrels, Allen Karsh, Tony Litschewski, Bruno Marino, Bob McConnell, Michael Mauro, Aileen Maxwell, Jack Olson, John Penrod, Lou Poulter, Ron Ruhoff, Jamie Schwaberow, Rodger Shiflet, Glenn W. Swan, Fred Wangaard, Joe Weinberger.

Text by: Carolyn and Fred Wangaard; Ron Ruhoff

Demographics by: AAA Colorado, Utah Tour-Book 3/07

Edited by: Rich Swan, Bill Kallio

Published by:
Sanborn Ltd.
8571 Rosemary St.
Commerce City, CO 80037